THE OLYMPIC GAMES

STICKER BOOK

In association with
The Olympic Museum

Susan Meredith

Illustrated by Galia Bernstein
Designed by Tom Lalonde

CONTENTS

How the Games Began

The Olympic Games is the biggest multi-sport event in the world. No one is quite sure how they began, but the first recorded Games took place in ancient Greece almost 3,000 years ago. They were held every four years – just as they are today.

The Games take their name from the place where they were held – Olympia, a beautiful spot where people went to worship Zeus, king of the Greek gods. The Games were held in his honour.

Visitors flocked to the Games in increasing numbers after a magnificent temple was built at Olympia.

The temple contained a statue of Zeus said to be a huge 13m (43ft) high.

This is how the temple might have looked when it was first built.

A 19th-century illustration of the statue of Zeus at Olympia

To honour Zeus, a flame was kept burning day and night. For the modern Games, a torch is lit at Olympia and carried in a relay all the way to the host city.

The Games were about more than sport and religion. Every Olympiad – four year period – a temporary truce was called between the warring city states of Greece so that people could travel safely to the next Games.

Messengers told soldiers to lay down their arms.

At modern lighting-the-torch ceremonies, actors play the role of ancient Greek priestesses.

Equestrian events consisted of chariot racing as well as horse racing.

The very first Games had only one event – a running race. But the competition expanded until it lasted five days, with events in long jump, shot put, javelin, discus, equestrian, boxing, wrestling, pankration, and even a race in armour.

Except for charioteers, the athletes had to compete naked, as the Greeks felt they should show off their strong and beautiful bodies.

Only men could compete. Married women were not even allowed to watch – on pain of death.

A statue of a discus thrower at the ancient Games

Pankration was a brutal mixture of boxing and wrestling with only two rules – no biting and no eye gouging.

Long jumpers didn't do a run-up but jumped from a standing start. To help them jump further, they swung weights forwards and backwards, for momentum.

At the ancient Games, winners were crowned with a wreath of olive leaves. This tradition was revived for the Athens Games of 2004, when winners were given a wreath as well as medals.

By the year 393, Greece was under Roman rule and Emperor Theodosius I banned the Games. His soldiers destroyed the temple, Olympia fell into ruins, and there were no more Games for over 1,500 years.

The medal winners of the women's artistic gymnastics floor exercises, 2004

Emperor Theodosius I

THE GAMES ARE REVIVED

Over the centuries, Olympia was buried by earthquakes and floods. But after archaeologists rediscovered it, there was a huge surge of interest in the ancient Games which led to the founding of the modern competition in 1896.

In 1875, the remains of temples, sculptures and pots were unearthed at a big archaeological dig at Olympia led by German archaeologist Ernst Curtius.

Inspired by the rediscovery of Olympia, French nobleman and keen sportsman Baron Pierre de Coubertin had the idea of reviving the Games.

Pierre de Coubertin

Cycle racing at the Much Wenlock Olympian Games of the 1870s

A multi-sport festival called the Much Wenlock Olympian Games was being held regularly in the small English town of Much Wenlock. De Coubertin went to watch to get ideas.

Finally, in 1894, he managed to form the International Olympic Committee (IOC) and organize the first modern Games, to be held in Athens. The IOC is still in charge of the Games today.

At this early meeting of the IOC, de Coubertin is second from the right.

De Coubertin used to say that the most important thing at the Games – and in life too – was not the winning but the taking part.

SCRIBNER'S

The Olympic Games and their Revival

Stories

Lord Leighton

Cathode Photography

Quarrel of the English Speaking Peoples

APRIL

A magazine advertises the 1896 Games with an ancient Greek warrior.

At Athens 1896, more than 200 male athletes from 14 countries competed in nine different sports: athletics, cycling, fencing, gymnastics, shooting, swimming, tennis, weightlifting and wrestling.

The start of the 100m race in 1896

Swimming events weren't held in a pool, so competitors had to dive out of a boat and race through the cold, rough sea.

The first Olympic champion since the ancient Games was an American called James Connolly. He spent almost all his savings on the 17-day boat journey to Europe, but won the hop, step and jump (now called the triple jump).

The marathon race was invented for the 1896 Games. It was inspired by a story about an ancient Greek soldier, Pheidippides, who ran about 40km (25 miles) from the town of Marathon to Athens, with the news that the Greeks had beaten the Persians in battle.

James Connolly with the flag of the USA

The Greek spectators were delighted when their entrant for the marathon, a shepherd called Spyridon Louis, stormed to victory well ahead of anyone else.

Spyridon Louis wore Greek national dress at the medals ceremony.

The Greek king's sons, who were watching, were so excited that they jumped onto the track and ran with Spyridon to the finishing line.

THE GAMES DEVELOP

Athens 1896 was so successful that it was decided to hold the Games every four years, like in ancient Greece, but in a different country each time.

1900

The Olympic Games of 1900 took place in Paris, at the insistence of de Coubertin. This time, women could take part, though only in 'ladylike' sports such as tennis, golf and croquet.

British tennis player Charlotte Cooper was the first women's Olympic champion in an individual event.

1904

The 1904 Games, in St Louis, USA, were held to coincide with a trade fair. But they were poorly attended because athletes couldn't afford to make the long journey to America from other continents.

A programme cover for the 1904 Olympic Games and World's Fair

1908

At the London Games of 1908, the length of the marathon was altered slightly so the king and queen could watch the start from their windows at Windsor Castle. The marathon is now always 42.195km (26 miles 385 yards).

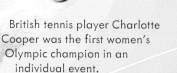

Dorando Pietri of Italy was declared the marathon winner, but was later disqualified because he'd been helped over the finishing line, exhausted.

1912

In 1912, in Stockholm, an electronic timer and finishing line camera were used for the first time at a Games. There was also a public address system.

At Stockholm, one wrestling match lasted over 11 hours – that's the longest wrestling bout ever recorded.

It was hard to see who came second and who third in the 1500m of 1912. A finishing line camera proved it.

1924

Following a Winter Sports Week in 1924, the IOC decided that separate Games should be held for winter sports, in the same year as the main Games. To differentiate between the two, they became known as the Olympic Summer Games and Olympic Winter Games.

PARIS · LYON · MÉDITERRANÉE

CHAMONIX-MONT BLANC
TOUTES LES INSTALLATIONS DE SPORTS D'HIVER

A poster for the 1924 Winter Games

1928

In 1928, at the Amsterdam Games, women were finally allowed to compete in athletics and gymnastics. But the all-male organizers soon decided that long races were too 'dangerous' for women.

Male officials were so shocked to see women looking exhausted after the 800m that they banned them from any race over 200m – for over 30 years.

1932

The first complete Olympic village was built for athletes attending the Los Angeles Games of 1932. It included a hospital and a bank, as well as accommodation. Only the men lived in the village. The women stayed in a hotel.

1960

In Rome, in 1960, the first Paralympic Games were held for disabled athletes. Later, in 1976, the Paralympic Winter Games began. They are held immediately after the main Games.

The wheelchair javelin event at the 1960 Paralympic Games

2010

In 2010, in Singapore, the first Youth Olympic Games were held, for 14-18 year olds. These broadly follow the format of the adult Games and, like them, are held every four years.

The first gold medalist was Yuka Sato of Japan in the girls' triathlon – a 750m (0.47 mile) swim, followed by a 20km (12 mile) cycle and a 5km (3.1 mile) run.

THE VENUES

It takes so long to prepare for an Olympic Games that the IOC chooses a host city seven years in advance. Many buildings are specially designed and constructed for the Games.

The main Olympic site is known as the Olympic Park. It is self-contained, covers a large area, and has green spaces as well as buildings.

Olympic stadium
The main, large stadium where athletics events and opening and closing ceremonies are held.

Aquatics centre
For swimming, diving, synchronized swimming and sometimes water polo.

Smaller stadiums
For various different events.

Some events are held off-site, if they require rough country terrain or large areas of water, for instance.

Mountain biking near Athens, 2004

Windsurfing in Sydney harbour, 2000

Existing venues are sometimes used, if they are suitable.

In 2012, 5,000 tonnes of sand was brought in so that beach volleyball could be held on a big royal parade ground in central London.

Some parks and arenas are designed so they will still be useful after the Games.

The Beijing 2008 aquatics centre is now a waterpark with slides and wave machines.

Velodrome
Where track cycling events are held.

Press centre
For the thousands of broadcasters, photographers and journalists from around the world.

Transport links often have to be modernised to cope with the huge numbers of visitors to the Games.

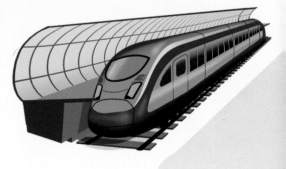

The Games couldn't take place without thousands of volunteers. They work, unpaid, to help the Games run smoothly, for example by directing people.

Athletes' village
This is usually on-site. As well as sleeping accommodation, it includes restaurants, shops and medical facilities, to make life more convenient for the athletes.

THE SPORTS

There are currently 28 sports at the Summer Games, chosen by the IOC. Some are split into different 'disciplines', and medals are given for each 'event' within a sport or discipline.

Only five sports have been included in every Summer Games since 1896: athletics, swimming, gymnastics, cycling and fencing.

One event to be dropped was the tug-of-war, on the programme from 1900 to 1920.

Archery was reintroduced in 1972 after being dropped for over 50 years. High-tech modern arrows can travel at over 240km (150 miles) an hour.

Many people consider Soo-Nyung Kim of South Korea the greatest female archer ever. She won her first gold medals in 1988, aged only 17.

Shooting events are divided into three groups: rifle, pistol and shotgun.

Shooting with rifles

Fencing began as a type of military training. Events are held using three different types of swords: foil, epée and sabre. French and Italian fencers have won the most medals.

In 1920, Italian Nedo Nadi (left) won gold in every weapon – a record for a single Games which still stands today.

Weightlifting takes place in groups according to the lifters' bodyweight. In women's weightlifting, introduced in 2000, Chinese lifters have won the most golds.

Pyrros Dimas of Greece is the weightlifter with the most Olympic medals – three golds and a bronze.

Equestrian began as a way of training horses for the battlefield. It's divided into three disciplines: jumping, dressage and eventing.

In jumping, riders take their horses over a course of obstacles, such as fences, hedges and water.

In dressage, riders demonstrate how well they can get their horses to follow instructions. Eventing combines dressage, jumping and a demanding cross-country course.

Equestrian is the only Olympic sport in which men and women compete against each other in individual events.

Isabell Werth and her horse Gigolo are one of the most successful pairings in the history of dressage.

Modern pentathlon consists of five events, held in one day. First, contestants fence one another; next they swim 200m freestyle, then jump a horse around a course. Finally, three times over, they must shoot at five targets and run 1000m.

Triathlon has been an Olympic event since 2000. Triathletes first swim 1500m, then cycle 40km and finally run 10km.

The women's combined shooting and running event in 2012. Laura Asadauskaite of Lithuania (right) set a new Olympic record.

Pentathlon was a highlight of the ancient Games, where the five sports were long jump, javelin, discus, running and wrestling. The winner was crowned 'victor of the Games'.

British brothers Alistair and Jonathan Brownlee running in the triathlon in 2012

Alistair (right) won gold and Jonathan bronze.

ATHLETICS

Athletics plays a key role in the Games as it has since ancient times. There are currently 47 events – more than for any other sport – but it isn't broken down into different disciplines.

Races are held on the track round the edge of the stadium. Other events are held on the 'field' in the middle.

There are over 30 different races. These are either short sprints (100m, 200m and 400m), middle distance (800m, 1500m and 3000m) or long distance (5000m, 10000m, the marathon and the race walks).

Field events consist of jumping: the highest in high jump; the longest in long jump and triple jump; throwing the furthest in discus, hammer, javelin and shot put; or vaulting the highest in pole vault.

Javier Sotomayor of Cuba won Olympic high jump gold in 1992. In 1993, he cleared 2.45m (8ft), a world record which still stands today.

In 2012, Usain Bolt of Jamaica became the first man to achieve a 'double double', successfully defending both his Olympic 100m and 200m titles.

The ultimate athletics tests are the decathlon (10 different track and field events) for men and heptathlon (seven events) for women. The winners are often known as 'the world's greatest athletes'.

Jessica Ennis of Great Britain hurdling in the 2012 heptathlon. She won heptathlon gold.

In the hammer event, contestants don't actually throw a hammer. They throw a metal ball attached to a handle.

AQUATICS

Aquatics is split into four disciplines – swimming, diving, water polo and synchronized swimming. Swimming and diving have the most events.

Swimming races are held in four strokes – freestyle, butterfly, backstroke and breaststroke. They can be as short as 50m (just one length of the pool) or as long as 10km (the marathon).

Michael Phelps of the USA swimming butterfly in 2008. His 22 medals (18 of them gold) make him the highest medal-winning Olympian of all time.

Water polo is a tough, fast team game, with the aim of scoring goals. The water is too deep for players to touch the bottom, so they may swim as far as 5km (over 3 miles) in a match.

Synchronized swimmers – women only at the Olympic Games – perform balletic routines to music, in sync with each other. They need incredible breath control because they are underwater a lot of the time.

Divers compete to perform the best dives from a 3m-high springboard or a 10m-high platform. In synchronized diving, two divers dive in sync with each other.

China's Guo Jingjing and Wu Minxia win gold in the women's synchronized 3m springboard, 2008.

Tamás Kásás of Hungary aims to get the ball past his Serbian-Montenegrin opponent in the men's water polo gold medal game, 2004. Hungary won.

Divers travel at up to 55kph (35mph). In synchronized diving it takes a large panel of up to 11 judges to score them.

BALLS, RACKETS AND STICKS

Over a third of the sports played at the Games are ball games, reflecting their popularity around the world.

Badminton is played with a shuttlecock – a piece of cork covered in goat skin with 16 goose feathers attached. Players from Asian countries have won almost 90% of the medals.

China (in red) beating South Korea in the badminton women's doubles final, 2008

Tennis made a comeback in 1988, after last being played at the Games back in 1924.

Steffi Graf of Germany winning the women's singles gold in 1988. She also won bronze in the women's doubles.

Li Huifen of China on her way to a silver medal in the women's singles, 1988

Table tennis is especially popular in China and Chinese players have won the most Olympic medals.

Golf was last played at the Games in 1904 and rugby in 1924, until both were reintroduced for Rio 2016.

Table tennis was invented in England as an after-dinner game, with players using whatever they could find for equipment.

Hockey at the Games is played on artificial turf which is softer, safer and faster than grass.

Germany (in white) beat the Netherlands in the 2012 final.

Basketball was invented in the USA as an alternative to outdoor ball games, for cold weather. US teams have won most golds.

Basketball really used to be played with a basket and the ball didn't drop through. It was several years before the baskets were replaced by hoops.

Volleyball was originally intended to be a less strenuous alternative to basketball.

The US team fails to stop a pass from gold medal winners China in the women's final, 1984.

An Argentinian player shoots against a Russian in 2012.

Beach volleyball began as a fun outdoor version of volleyball. Matches are shorter, because players have to cope with sand, sun and wind.

Football first appeared at the Olympic Games in 1900. Since 1996, African and South American teams have won all the men's gold medals.

A Norwegian handball player in the women's team's gold-medal-winning match against Russia, 2008

A Brazilian player (in yellow) tackles an Argentinian in 2008.

Handball is similar to football but played with the hands instead of the feet. At the Olympic Games today, it's played indoors.

GYMNASTICS

Gymnastics has been on the programme since the first modern Games of 1896. Today it is split into three disciplines: artistic, rhythmic and trampoline, with points awarded for technique and grace.

Artistic gymnasts perform breathtaking moves, including somersaults, leaps and balances, both on apparatus and the floor. Some of the apparatus is different for men and women.

Louis Smith of Great Britain on the pommel horse in 2012, when he won silver

London 2012

Seven-times Olympic gold medalist Vera Cáslávska of Czechoslovakia on the uneven bars in 1964

Rhythmic gymnastics is only done by women at the Games. They perform floor routines to music, including balances, spins and leaps, and incorporating hoops, ribbons, balls, ropes and clubs.

Trampoline has only been an Olympic discipline since 2000. Previously, trampolines were mainly used in training, by divers as well as gymnasts.

Evgeniya Kanaeva of Russia dances her way to all-round rhythmic gymnastics gold in 2008. In 2012, she became the first gymnast to win this medal for a second time.

In 1904 and 1932, a club-swinging event was held. Male gymnasts whirled clubs around as fast as they could, in complicated patterns.

Cycling

Cycling is one of the five sports on the programme at every Games since 1896. Today there are four disciplines: track, road, mountain bike and BMX.

The best performing Olympic cyclist of all time is Briton Chris Hoy, who has six gold medals.

There are two types of road event. In the road race everyone starts together, in a bunch, and first over the finish line wins. In the time trial, they start a minute or two apart and are individually timed.

Most cycling events take place on a track in the velodrome – an arena specially for cycling. The most challenging event is the omnium – six different races, both sprint and endurance, held over two days.

Dutch cyclist Leontien van Moorsel, who has four Olympic golds, leads the pack in the 2004 women's road race.

The longest-ever Olympic race of any kind was the cycling individual time trial in 1912. It was about 320km (200 miles) long and took over 10 hours.

BMX has been an Olympic event only since 2008. Cyclists race around a course full of bends, obstacles and jumps.

Mountain bike events take place over a rough cross-country course. The sport only developed after tough new bikes were invented.

Maris Strombergs of Latvia, who is known as 'The Machine', won BMX gold in both 2008 and 2012. Here, he takes the lead in a jump.

COMBAT SPORTS

There are four hand-to-hand combat sports at the Games.
Contestants fight in different groups, depending on their weight.

Wrestling has two disciplines. In Greco-Roman, done by men only, contestants can only fight with their arms and upper body. In freestyle, they can use and grab the legs as well. Freestyle is done by men and women.

Greco-Roman gold medalist Jung Ji-Hyun of South Korea topples Roberto Monzón of Cuba in the 2004 final.

Boxing at the Games only became open to women in 2012. Although punches to the head are allowed, from 2016 men will no longer wear helmets.

Nicola Adams of Great Britain became the first-ever female boxing gold medalist. Here she aims a punch at Ren Cancan of China.

Judo developed from jujitsu, a type of hand-to-hand combat done by samurai warriors in ancient Japan. Japanese judokas (people who do judo) have won most medals.

Ayumi Tanimoto of Japan throws Lucie Décosse of France on her way to a judo gold medal in 2008.

Taekwondo is an ancient Korean martial art whose trademark is its combination of kicking and punching. It became an Olympic sport in 2000.

At the ancient Games, there were no weight divisions, so the heavier fighter usually had the advantage.

Hadi Saei of Iran kicks his way towards gold in 2004 against Huang Chih-hsiung of Chinese Taipei.

ON THE WATER

Rowing, sailing and canoeing are the Olympic boat sports, with canoeing split into two disciplines.

Canoeing sprint events take place in flat water and competitors race straight for the finish. Canoeing slalom is held in steep whitewater rapids, and they have to weave around poles.

Slovakian twins Pavol and Peter Hochschorner battle the rapids in canoe slalom in 2012. They won bronze, but already had three previous golds.

Both canoeing sprint and canoeing slalom have separate events for canoes and kayaks. What's the difference?

Kayakers use double-bladed paddles and sit in their boats ...

... but canoeists use single-bladed paddles and kneel – on both knees in slalom, on one in sprint.

Rowing and sailing were on the Olympic programme as early as 1896 but had to be cancelled that year due to dangerously strong winds.

Sailing races are grouped by size and weight of boats. In general, boats are being made smaller and lighter, which means it takes greater skill and athleticism to control them in the wind.

Four-times gold medal winner Ben Ainslie of Great Britain manoeuvres his boat in 2004.

Rowing events are split into two types: sculls, where each rower has two oars, and sweep, where they only have one. Rowing events are the only ones done backwards, apart from backstroke swimming.

The Romanian women's team celebrate a gold in 2004. Elisabeta Lipa (fourth from left) has won more rowing medals than anyone else – five golds, two silver and one bronze.

THE WINTER GAMES

Today there are seven sports at the Winter Games, with almost a hundred events. From their introduction in 1924 until 1992 the Winter Games were held in the same year as the Summer Games. Now, they are two years later.

The separate winter competition was set up because the Games had grown very big – and it made more sense to hold snow and ice events in the cold.

Even in winter, there can be snow shortages. In 1964 the Austrian army had to take extra supplies to the Games at Innsbruck.

Many winter sports began in the cold countries of Scandinavia. At the 1924 Winter Games, athletes from Norway and Finland won more medals than all the other countries combined.

Norwegian skater Sonja Henie made her debut in 1924, aged only 11, going on to win gold medals at the next three Games.

Skating is the oldest Olympic winter sport. It is split into figure skating, including dancing, and speed skating (races).

Vladimir Grigorev of Russia ahead of Sin Da-woon of South Korea in the men's 1000m short track speed skating semi-final, 2014

Short track skaters always go anti-clockwise. Their blades are to the left so their boots don't scrape on the ice when they lean over.

Ice hockey originated in Canada and Canadian teams have won most Olympic medals. The game is played with a disc called a 'puck', instead of a ball.

Curling teams compete at sliding a heavy, polished 'rock' along a sheet of ice. They brush the ice with brooms to help the rock move along.

A Canadian player (in red) fights for the puck with a Swede in the women's ice hockey final, 2006. Canada won gold.

Lui Yin of the Chinese women's team slides the rock in their bronze-medal-winning match, 2010.

Skiing has the most events. It is split into several types of races, some including jumps, and 'freestyle' events, judged on how acrobatic they are. Freestylers perform jumps, twists and flips, up to 20m (over 65ft) off the ground.

Dara Howell of Canada leaps her way to gold in a women's freestyle skiing event, 2014.

Snowboarding – a sport taken up by several surfers and skateboarders – is the newest skiing discipline, introduced in 1998.

Ina Meschik of Austria weaves around a flag in the women's snowboard parallel slalom, 2014.

Biathlon combines cross-country skiing with rifle shooting. It started in Scandinavia, where people used to go hunting through the snow on skis.

Bobsleigh and **luge** athletes make superfast, timed runs down a narrow, twisting ice track.

Bobsleighers sit in a sled which they steer by pulling on ropes. But luges and bobsleigh 'skeletons' have no seats or steering and competitors lie on them.

The French four-man bobsleigh team compete at Albertville, France, in 1992.

Athletes push a skeleton, at a run, then jump onto it on their stomachs and go head first.

On a luge, athletes lie on their backs and travel feet first. There is a men's doubles luge event, in which one athlete lies on top of the other.

21

THE PARALYMPIC GAMES

The second-biggest multi-sport event in the world, after the Olympic Games, the Paralympic Games are for top athletes who have a disability. The Games are organized by the International Paralympic Committee (IPC).

The Games were the idea of a doctor, Ludwig Guttmann, who believed his severely injured patients would benefit from exercise. In 1948, he organized a wheelchair archery competition at his hospital – Stoke Mandeville, in England.

Doctor Ludwig Guttmann

The Stoke Mandeville Games expanded and became an annual event, developing into the first Paralympic Games in Rome, in 1960. Until 1976, they were for wheelchair athletes only.

In Rome, 400 athletes competed, from 23 countries. By London 2012, there were over 4,200, from 164 countries. Now, there are 10 different disability categories, with athletes divided into groups within the categories, according to their level of disability.

Aerial performers at the opening ceremony for the Paralympic Games in 2012

This is blade runner April Holmes of the USA in the 2012 women's 100m, when she won bronze.

There are over 20 sports and more than 500 events at the Summer Games. As at the Olympic Games, most events are in athletics and swimming.

The Paralympic flag

The Paralympic symbol was designed to indicate movement. The motto is 'Spirit in motion' and the word 'paralympic' means 'parallel to the Olympic Games'.

Powerlifting, and wheelchair sports, such as basketball, fencing, rugby and tennis, require incredible strength in the upper body.

Powerlifters lift weights lying down on a specially designed bench.

Goalball is for visually impaired and blind athletes. Players score by rolling a ball into the opponents' goal. The ball has a bell inside so they can hear where it is. Wearing masks means no one has an unfair advantage.

Esther Vergeer of the Netherlands has won gold in the women's wheelchair tennis at four separate Paralympic Games.

The Japanese women's team in action in their gold-medal-winning match against China in 2012

A visually impaired athlete is allowed a sighted guide in some sports. In races, they run together, attached at the wrist; in skiing, a sighted skier goes in front giving instructions over a wireless connection.

In cycling, a sighted 'pilot' sits in front of a non-sighted athlete on a tandem.

The first Paralympic Winter Games were held at Örnsköldsvik, Sweden, in 1976. Today, there are six sports and over 70 events – most in skiing, which can be done sitting or standing.

Bronze medalist Allison Jones of the USA in the women's downhill standing skiing event, 2014

Jones is using two 'outriggers' – a cross between a pole and a crutch with a small ski at the bottom.

Ice sledge hockey players sit on a double-bladed sledge, which takes the place of skates. They use two sticks, which have a spike at one end for propelling them around the ice.

A Swedish player (in yellow) races for the puck during a men's Sweden versus Italy match in 2014.

OPENING AND CLOSING CEREMONIES

Ceremonies celebrate the peaceful spirit of the Games and honour the achievements of the athletes. In recent years they have become more and more spectacular.

The opening ceremony for Beijing 2008 was especially lavish. Over 15,000 actors, dancers and musicians enacted the history of China under the motto 'One world, one dream'. The show ended with thousands of dazzling fireworks.

Exactly 2,008 drummers took part in the 2008 opening ceremony.

A dancer at the Beijing 2008 opening ceremony

After the displays, the athletes parade into the stadium. Greece enters first, the host country last, and the others in alphabetical order. It can take nearly two hours for them all to get in.

After the host country's head of state declares the Games open, the Olympic flag is carried in and raised, while the Olympic hymn is played. Then a solemn oath is taken.

The Olympic symbol of five rings, shown on the flag, represents the union of the five inhabited continents. At least one of the colours appears on the flag of every country.

An athlete, a judge and a coach from the host country, representing all the rest, swear an Olympic oath – a promise to abide by the rules and behave in a spirit of sportsmanship.

A highlight of the ceremony is when the Olympic torch, brought all the way from Athens, is carried into the stadium and used to light the Olympic cauldron. The cauldron is kept burning day and night during the Games.

In 2012, the cauldron was made of 204 copper petals, one for each nation competing.

The torch used at the 1998 Winter Games in Japan

At the Winter Games of 1994, Norwegian ski jumper Stein Gruben carried the torch into the stadium down a steep ski slope. He even did a ski jump on the way.

Acrobats forming a dove shape at the opening of the 2006 Winter Games

Doves represent peace, so dove symbols are a feature of opening ceremonies.

At closing ceremonies, there are artistic displays and lots of fireworks, but the athletes can come into the stadium all mixed up together and there is more of a party atmosphere than at opening ceremonies.

The closing ceremony, 2012

MEDALS

Medals were first given in 1896, when the winner received a silver medal, and the runner-up copper.

The 1896 medals showed Zeus, holding a globe, symbolizing the world. The goddess Nike holds an olive branch, for peace.

Recent Olympic medals are about as big as a jamjar lid. Gold medals are actually made of silver, covered with gold. For the Summer Games the medals must show Nike, Greek goddess of victory.

Nike on the 2008 gold medal

The medal for the 1988 Winter Games in Canada showed a Native American wearing a headdress of winter sports equipment.

The 2014 Paralympic Winter Games medals were unusual in having decorated glassy 'crystals' set into the metal. Sochi is written in braille at the bottom.

In the early 1900s, athletes and officials dressed in their smartest clothes for medals ceremonies.

A special trophy for fair play, named after Pierre de Coubertin, is awarded only occasionally, to athletes who show exceptional sportsmanship.

The first was given in 1964 to Italian bobsledder Eugenio Monti.

Since 1932, athletes have stood on a podium at medals ceremonies, with the winner in the middle, the runner up on their right and the third place competitor on their left.

Lena Schöneborn of Germany celebrates her gold for the 2008 modern pentathlon.

Silver medalist Heather Fell of Great Britain

Bronze medalist Victoria Tereshuk of Ukraine

Monti generously gave his British rivals an axle bolt because theirs had broken. The Britons went on to win, with the Italians coming third.

MASCOTS AND EMBLEMS

The best-known Olympic symbol is the five rings. But each individual Games also has its own mascot, emblem and pictograms.

Mascots are usually animals connected to the Games' host country.

The first official mascot was made for the Munich Games of 1972. 'Waldi' was a dachshund – a popular dog in southern Germany, known for its endurance and agility.

Native Americans see otters as a very powerful animal. So 'Otto' was chosen as mascot for the Paralympic Winter Games in Salt Lake City, 2002.

At the end of the 1980 Summer Games in Moscow, a giant 'Misha the Bear' mascot was released from the stadium dangling from balloons. He landed safely on a hill a few hours later.

Emblems are used in advertising for the Games. They must include the Olympic rings symbol.

The Seoul 1988 emblem was based on a traditional pattern, seen all over South Korea. It is often used to decorate fans.

SEOUL 1988

NAGANO
1 9 9 8

A flower, with the petals representing athletes, formed the Nagano Winter Games emblem. It can also be seen as a snowflake.

Pictograms are symbols that must be easy to see and understand, no matter what language a person speaks. Olympic pictograms are used to help people find their way around venues.

Rugby pictogram 2016

Mascots and emblems feature on the mass of souvenirs made for each Games, and on the special postage stamps that are produced.

The emblem for Rio 2016 shows three people holding hands in colours associated with Brazil – blue (sea), yellow (sun), green (forest).

Rio2016™

The designer also included the shape of Rio's famous Sugar Loaf Mountain.

London 2012 emblem on a toy bus

POSTERS

A whole range of posters is produced for each Games, advertising the sports, cultural events and the host country.

The first official poster was designed for the 1912 Games. The naked athlete – a reference to the ancient Games – caused shock, and the poster was even banned in China.

The first poster to include the Olympic rings was in 1928. The striking design combines the Olympic flag, the flag of Switzerland – the host country – and a snowy Swiss mountain.

In the early days, people had to rely on posters and newspapers for information about the Games because they didn't have radios and televisions.

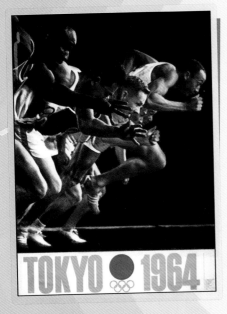

A poster for the 1900 Games showed a female fencer, even though women didn't compete in fencing until 1924.

This photograph was taken on an icy cold night in Japan and took over 60 attempts to get right. The runners were amateur American and Japanese athletes.

Sometimes famous artists are commissioned to design posters. This one, advertising diving events in 1972, is by David Hockney.

This bold, modern design advertised the Paralympic Winter Games in 2014. The athlete is an ice sledge hockey player.

Competitions are usually held to select poster designs. The organizers brief the designers beforehand on the kind of things they would like to see.

A series of 28 posters combining photographs of the Earth and athletes in dramatic poses was produced for the 1992 Games. Here, an athlete does a high jump.

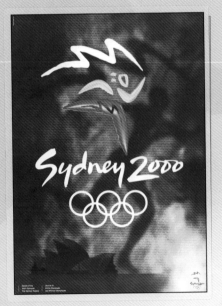

In this poster, the athlete is made up of boomerangs and the torch is in the shape of the Sydney Opera House. The blue background is intended to make people think of the blue sky and sea of Australia.

Posters can boost tourism by making people want to see a country's sights as well as the Games.

The Olympic marathon at London 2012

This poster advertises the Moscow Games of 1980. A hand in the colours of the Olympic rings holds an Olympic torch. The background shows the Moscow skyline.

FASTER, HIGHER, STRONGER

Adopted by Pierre de Coubertin, 'Faster, higher, stronger' is one of the mottos of the Olympic Games. Here are some of the amazing records that have been achieved.

SUMMER GAMES

Most medals (men): 22
Michael Phelps (USA)
for aquatics (swimming), 2004-2012. 18 of these were gold, which makes Phelps the gold medal record holder too.

Most medals (women): 18
Larisa Latynina (USSR)
for gymnastics, 1956-1964. 9 of these were gold, which makes her the women's gold medal record holder as well.

Most gold medals at the same Games (men): 8
Michael Phelps (USA)
for aquatics (swimming), 2008

Most gold medals at the same Games (women): 6
Kristin Otto (German Democratic Republic)
for aquatics (swimming), 1988

Youngest known medalist: 10 years old
Dimitrios Loundras (Greece)
for gymnastics (team bronze in parallel bars), 1896

Larisa Latynina

Youngest gold medalist in an individual event: 13 years old
Marjorie Gestring (USA)
for aquatics (3m springboard diving), 1936

Oldest medalist: 72 years old
Oscar Swahn (Sweden)
for shooting (team silver in running deer double shots), 1920

Oscar Swahn

Most Games participations: 10
Ian Millar (Canada)
in equestrian, 1972-2012

Ian Millar

In 1900 an unknown French boy acted as coxswain for a pair of Dutch rowers and they won gold. Afterwards he disappeared but could have been as young as 7.

Biggest stadium: 110,000 seats
Sydney, 2000

Most volunteers: hundreds of thousands
Beijing, 2008

WINTER GAMES

Most medals (men): 13
Ole Einar Bjørndalen (Norway)
for biathlon, 1994-2014

Most medals (women): 10 each
Raisa Smetanina (USSR)
for skiing (cross-country), 1976-1992
Stefania Belmondo (Italy)
for skiing (cross-country), 1992-2002
Marit Bjørgen (Norway)
for skiing (cross-country), 2002-2014

Youngest medalist in an
individual event: 14 years old
Scott Allen (USA)
for figure skating (bronze), 1964

Youngest gold medalist in
an individual event: 15 years old
Tara Lipinski (USA)
for figure skating, 1998

Ole Einar Bjørndalen

PARALYMPIC GAMES

Most medals (men): 21
Michael Edgson (Canada)
including 18 golds, for visually-
impaired swimming, 1984-1992

Most medals (women): 55
Trischa Zorn (USA)
including 41 golds, for blind
swimming, 1980-2004

Youngest Paralympian: 11 years old
Natalia Partyka (Poland)
limb deficient table tennis, 2000

Trischa Zorn

PARALYMPIC WINTER GAMES

Most medals (men): 22
Gerd Schoenfelder (Germany)
including 16 golds, for amputee alpine
skiing, 1992-2010

Most medals (women): 27
Ragnhild Myklebust (Norway)
one for every event she ever entered,
including 22 golds, for sit-ski cross-
country skiing, ice sledge speed
racing and biathlon, 1988-2002

Ragnhild
Myklebust

GAMES DATES AND VENUES

Summer Games

1896 Athens, Greece
1900 Paris, France
1904 St Louis, USA
1908 London, Great Britain
1912 Stockholm, Sweden
1920 Antwerp, Belgium
1924 Paris, France
1928 Amsterdam, Netherlands
1932 Los Angeles, USA
1936 Berlin, Germany
1948 London, Great Britain
1952 Helsinki, Finland
1956 Melbourne, Australia
1960 Rome, Italy
1964 Tokyo, Japan
1968 Mexico City, Mexico
1972 Munich, Federal Republic
      of Germany
1976 Montreal, Canada
1980 Moscow, USSR
1984 Los Angeles, USA
1988 Seoul, South Korea
1992 Barcelona, Spain
1996 Atlanta, USA
2000 Sydney, Australia
2004 Athens, Greece
2008 Beijing, China
2012 London, Great Britain
2016 Rio de Janeiro, Brazil
2020 Tokyo, Japan

In 1956 equestrian
events had to be
held in Stockholm
because of strict
quarantine laws
in Australia.

Games were not held in 1916, 1940
and 1944 because of the World Wars.

Winter Games

1924 Chamonix, France
1928 St Moritz, Switzerland
1932 Lake Placid, USA
1936 Garmisch-Partenkirchen, Germany
1948 St Moritz, Switzerland
1952 Oslo, Norway
1956 Cortina d'Ampezzo, Italy
1960 Squaw Valley, USA
1964 Innsbruck, Austria
1968 Grenoble, France
1972 Sapporo, Japan
1976 Innsbruck, Austria
1980 Lake Placid, USA
1984 Sarajevo, Yugoslavia
1988 Calgary, Canada
1992 Albertville, France
1994 Lillehammer, Norway
1998 Nagano, Japan
2002 Salt Lake City, USA
2006 Turin, Italy
2010 Vancouver, Canada
2014 Sochi, Russian Federation
2018 Pyeongchang, South Korea
2022 Beijing, China

In 2014 Russian
cosmonauts took
an Olympic torch
– unlit – for a
spacewalk on its
way to Sochi.

Usborne Quicklinks

For links to websites where you can find out more about the Olympic Games, go to
www.usborne.com/quicklinks and type the keywords **Olympic Games Sticker Book**.

Acknowledgements

Every effort has been made to trace and acknowledge ownership of copyright. If any rights have been omitted, the publishers offer to rectify this in any future editions following notification. The publishers are grateful to the following individuals and organizations for their permission to reproduce material on the following pages:

Cover: Olympic stadium during opening ceremony, London 2012 © Jamie Squire / Getty Images.
p.1: Chris Hoy © Ian MacNicol / Getty Images; Evgenia Kanaeva © Lluis Gene / AFP / Getty Images.
p.2: Statue of Zeus at Oympia, English School (20th century) / Private Collection / © Look and Learn / Bridgeman Images; Lighting-the-torch ceremony © Jamie McDonald / Getty Images.
p.3: Statue of discus thrower © The Trustees of the British Museum; Gymnastics medalists © 2004 Kishimoto / IOC / Nagaya, Yo; Theodosius I © Chronicle / Alamy Stock Photo.
p.4: Pierre de Coubertin © STR / Keystone / Corbis; Meeting of International Olympic Committee © 1896 International Olympic Committee (IOC) / Meyer, Albert; Magazine cover © 1896 International Olympic Committee (IOC).
p.5: Start of 100m race © 1896 International Olympic Committee (IOC); James Connolly © 1896 International Olympic Committee (IOC) / Meyer, Albert; Spyridon Louis © 1896 International Olympic Committee (IOC).
p.6: Charlotte Cooper © Popperfoto / Getty Images; World's Fair programme © 1904 International Olympic Committee (IOC); 1500m race © 1912 International Olympic Committee (IOC).
p.7: Chamonix poster © 1924 International Olympic Committee (IOC); Yuka Sato © 2010 Kishimoto / IOC / Mifune, Takamitsu.
p.8: Mountain biking © 2004 International Olympic Committee (IOC) / Sugimoto, Hiroki; Windsurfing © Bob Martin / Sports Illustrated / Getty Images.
p.9: Horse Guards Parade, London © Ezra Shaw / Getty Images; Aquatics centre, Beijing © AFP / AFP / Getty Images.
p.10: Nedo Nadi © Bettmann / CORBIS; Soo-Nyung Kim © International Olympic Committee (IOC); Pyrros Dimas © Al Bello / Getty Images.
p.11: Isabell Werth © Henri Szwarc / Bongarts / Getty Images; Pentathletes shooting © Alex Livesey / Getty Images; Brownlee Brothers © Tim Wimborne / Reuters / Corbis.
p.12: Usain Bolt © epa european pressphoto agency b.v. / Alamy Stock Photo; Javier Sotomayor © John Biever / Sports Illustrated / Getty Images; Jessica Ennis © Stu Forster / Getty Images.
p.13: Michael Phelps © Ezra Shaw / Getty Images; Water polo players © Daniel Berehulak / Getty Images for FINA; Guo Jingjing and Wu Minxia © Helen H. Richardson / The Denver Post via Getty Images.
p.14: Badminton match © 2008 International Olympic Committee (IOC) / Kishimoto, Tsutomu; Steffi Graf © 2015 International Olympic Committee (IOC) / United Artists; Li Huifen © 2013 International Olympic Committee (IOC) / United Archives; Hockey players © Rolf Vennenbernd / epa / Corbis.
p.15: Basketball players © Victor Caivano / AP / Press Association Images; Volleyball players © 1984 International Olympic Committee (IOC) / United Archives; Footballers © Clive Rose / Getty Images; Handball player © Lars Baron / Bongarts / Getty Images.
p.16: Louis Smith © Alan Edwards / Alamy Stock Photo; Vera Cáslavská © 1964 Kishimoto / IOC; Evgenia Kanaeva © Harry How / Getty Images.
p.17: Chris Hoy © Cameron Spencer / Getty Images; Leontien van Moorsel © Pool / Reuters / Corbis; Maris Strombergs © Stephane Reix / For Picture / Corbis.
p.18: Jung Ji-Hyun and Roberto Monzón © Doug Pensinger / Getty Images; Nicola Adams and Ren Cancan © Scott Heavey / Getty Images; Ayumi Tanimoto and Lucie Décosse © Lars Baron / Bongarts / Getty Images; Hadi Saei and Huang Chih-hsiung © Kim Kyung-Hoon / Reuters / Corbis.
p.19: Hochschorner twins © John Biever / Sports Illustrated / Getty Images; Ben Ainslie © Adam Pretty / Getty Images; Romanian rowers © Alexander Hassenstein / Bongarts / Getty Images.
p.20: Sonja Henie © 1924 International Olympic Committee (IOC) / Couttet, Auguste; Vladimir Grigorev and Sin Da-woon © Paul Gilham / Getty Images; Ice hockey players © Brian Bahr / Getty Images; Lui Yin © 2010 International Olympic Committee (IOC) / Evans, Jason.
p.21: Dara Howell © Cameron Spencer / Getty Images; Ina Meschik © 2014 International Olympic Committee (IOC) / Jones, Ian; French bobsleigh team © 1992 International Olympic Committee (IOC) / Strahm, Jean-Jacques.
p.22: Aerial performers © Dan Kitwood / Getty Images; April Holmes © Michael Steele / Getty Images; Paralympic symbol © International Paralympic Committee (IPC).
p.23: Esther Vergeer © Brian Bahr / Getty Images; Goalball players © Dennis Grombkowski / Getty Images; Allison Jones © Vassil Donev / epa / Corbis; Ice sledge hockey players © Harry Engels / Getty Images.
p.24: Beijing 2008 opening ceremony drummers, and dancer © 2008 International Olympic Committee (IOC) / Huet, John.
p.25: 2012 Olympic cauldron © David Eulitt / Kansas City Star / MCT via Getty Images; 1998 Olympic torch © 1998 International Olympic Committee (IOC); Dove athletes © Tony Bock / Toronto Star via Getty Images; London 2012 closing ceremony © Jamie Squire / Getty Images.
p.26: 1896, 2008 and 1988 medals © 1896, 2008 and 1988 International Olympic Committee (IOC); 2014 medal © RIA Novosti; Athletes on podium © A9312 Marcus Brandt / dpa / Corbis.
p.27: 1972 mascot, 1988, 1998 and 2016 emblems, 2016 pictogram, and toy London bus © 1972, 1988, 1998 and 2016, 2016 and 2012 International Olympic Committee (IOC); 2002 mascot © International Paralympic Committee (IPC);
p.28-29: 1912, 1928, 1964, 1992, 2000 and 1980 posters, and female fencer © 1912, 1928, 1964, 1992, 2000 and 1980 International Olympic Committee (IOC); David Hockney 'Munich Olympic Games' 1972 poster © David Hockney; 2014 poster © International Paralympic Committee (IPC).
p.30: Larisa Latynina © The Asahi Shimbun via Getty Images; Ian Millar © John MacDougall / AFP / GettyImages; Sydney stadium © Philippe Caron / Sygma / Corbis; Beijing volunteers © Troy Wayrynen / ZUMA Press / Corbis.
p.31: Ole Einar Bjørndalen © Shaun Botterill / Getty Images; Trischa Zorn © Aris Messinis / AFP / Getty Images; Ragnhild Myklebust © Matthew Stockman / Getty Images.

The Olympic properties, such as the Olympic symbol and the Olympic Heritage emblem, are the exclusive property of the IOC. TM / © International Olympic Committee. All images with © International Olympic Committee (IOC) – all rights reserved.

With thanks to Tony Collins and Ruth King. Cover design: Stephen Moncrieff.

HOW THE GAMES BEGAN

THE GAMES ARE REVIVED

THE GAMES ARE REVIVED (continued)
pages 4-5

THE GAMES DEVELOP
pages 6-7

THE VENUES
pages 8-9